LEGEND OF THE RECENT PAST

Books by James Haug

Legend of the Recent Past
Walking Liberty
The Stolen Car

Limited Editions

A Plan of How to Catch Amanda
Fox Luck

LEGEND OF THE RECENT PAST

poems

James Haug

The National Poetry Review Press
Aptos, California

The National Poetry Review Press
(an imprint of DHP)
Post Office Box 2080, Aptos, California 95001-2080

Printed in the United States of America
Published in 2009 by The National Poetry Review Press

978-0-9821155-4-1

Cover art piece:
"Equestrian Journey" by Michael Cutlip
www.michaelcutlip.com

for the boys

I found an old wide-awake hat and an old straw bonnet of the plum-pudding sort was left behind and I put the hat in my pocket thinking it might be useful for another opportunity and as good luck would have it, it turned out to be so.

—John Clare

Table of Contents

i.

Root Beer	15
Legend of the Recent Past	16
The Cop Is on the Settee	18
Gardner Exchange	19
Honest	20
Nostalgia for the Finite	22
Martina in the Badlands	23
How It Came to Be Connecticut	24
A Loft	25
Paradise City	26
Diorama	27
Big Rectangular Smile	28
44 in a School Zone	29
There's No Now	30

ii.

[place unknown]	35
A Plan of How to Catch Amanda	36
Also Known As	38
Wind Shear	40
Much Later	42
It's A Long Story So Let's Not Tell It	43
My Kind Is Unconnected	45
Idiot Means Good Luck	47
Cinco de Mayo, Virginia	49
Eeyore's Insomnia Rotisserie	51

Due West   52
Slept Here. Moved On.   53
Ghost 66   54

iii.
Accumulation   59
Everything's Jake   60
Livingston County   61
Eve with the Lid on   62
Spark Gap   64
A Day Unlike Any Other   65
Hard Times   66
Reconstruction   67
Leads   68
There   70
Bird Throat, Calabash, Glove Oil   71
Kind of a Strange Few Minutes   72
Lane of Blue Mist   74
Alberta Clipper   75
I've Got People in Town   76

i.

Root Beer

We found new combinations of interiors.
There was a painted door on the plains,
and a keyhole, and what we saw
was a fraction of what we suspected
could be found there. Some kind of floral
wallpaper covered everything. Brown water-
stains neatly suggested clouds resembling
segments of a traveling circus. I'm told
I saw a flea circus once, though I did not
actually see it, and now I have a disturbing
tendency to believe everything I hear.
When I head on home and repeat the facts,
my folks get fed up and send me out
into the yard. I'm standing out there now
with a pitchfork, trying to snag a low-
flying stormcloud that looks like Tolstoy,
fluffier than I remember him. I see
lightning hits near Jackson. My folks shake
their heads watching me from the kitchen.
Clouds swooping lower. Here comes that
circus, big cages on wheels, rumbling cumulo-
nimbus, which with my pitchfork I'll hook on
and swing aboard. Here I go, Celeste.

LEGEND OF THE RECENT PAST

I keep my shirt tucked because I don't
want everything falling out. I like
to arrive in one piece. I keep my nose
clean and almost never blow my top.
When I was young I was very tired.
I hung around police stations confessing
to muggings, shopliftings, second story jobs,
hoping to give the police a break,
maybe send them home for a nice rest.
You could say I wised-up. You could
say anything you want. I keep my boxes
straight, my lids tight, my pencils sharp.
It's almost like being in love. How
can I say that? I lived on the third floor
in a small town long long ago. And usually
around sunset I'd hear a voice, a small
croaky voice, an emphysemic gasping,
Someone's trying to kill me, which scared me
since it was right outside the window
and there was nowhere for a person,
even a little croaky person, to stand.
I ran down to the street and found
no one. I looked into open windows
in search of a loud TV, or maybe some guy
strangling in a curtain cord but nothing

did I find, except a cop who chased me
way away. So yonder I fled upstairs
to my rambling studio apartment, which had
no kitchen, but did have a sink and a stove
(if you must know) behind folding doors—
a Murphy kitchen, of all things.
And there at twilight I'd hang wet shirts
from a line stretched across the apartment
and stir myself a scalding cup of instant
while my wee friend Croaky rattled out
his nightly bit of worry, and I never
talked back, until one day I closed the door
with a suitcase full of shirts and boarded
a bus for a place known to many as Albany.

THE COP IS ON THE SETTEE

Woke today at the top of the world.
Not a Claude in the sky.
Forgot about the everyday horribles,
which surprised me.
If only I were in Europe again.
Europe has cathedrals.
Flying butlers.
Each morning I made a left turn
or a right turn,
lugging a ham sandwich down the boulevard.
I schlepped under the stars.
I was free because I knew nothing.
I could imagine people
wearing hats again. I wandered a bit
looped, like a marvelous traitor,
along the oldest riverbank in the West.
Derricks stooped for a drink.
Sit down, said a book dealer in his native tongue.
You look unusually tried.

Gardner Exchange

In a field I was overtaken by a conviction
that another field lay just beyond it.

Some ex-firemen had unfolded a card table
in the timothy, playing whist
where no other field was found.

In a town I sat like a clerk on a municipal bench
pretending I knew exactly where I was.

The streets long and straight.
I could see far away. I could see Orange.
For ten minutes I watched a woman approach by foot.

She handed me a handsome pamphlet
concerning the manufacture of chairs in this

the town I belonged to.

A siren reconfigured an old complaint.
How little I knew about rattan.
How perfectly useless the world's smallest chair looked

in my open hand.
I was the chair's chair.

Honest

Everyone complains about my appetite
but on Jupiter this grape weighs a ton.

I've got a Little Lady harmonica,
a fairy house of chicken bones.
I'm sleepy all day long.

When night-divers fall from the ether
I know where they land.

In June I finally learned to float.
I saved up a dozen Dixie cups.
A million miles for ants is a mile for us.

A hundred miles for us is a block for cowboys.

In a shoebox I've started my best
collection yet. It'll look like the world
under a lid.

Toads count on me.

Everyone says I sleep too little.
But I'm the biggest man in the yard

tonight—You better run
little arachnid. I have a list of everything
you've ever said in your whole life.

NOSTALGIA FOR THE FINITE

A dozen or so scale models are parked
under the windowsill, vintage
sports cars, German, English, tops down.
I used to hang my hand outside one
like that, I tell the Dead End Kids,
my *smoking* hand, and drop a lit one
while stopped at a red light. Every-
body knew my name, but not
a soul was saying. Gas was cheaper
then because it was miniature gas
and we never seemed to have to go
quite so far. It's not like things were
any closer, just standard practice
that you gave up going halfway there.
What I didn't know could fill I don't
know what. A secret anniversary
approaches, and a phalanx of tinhorns.
My favorite station runs tornado films
all night long. There's a song I'm dying
to hear except I forget how it goes.
I remember where I heard it, though
that place is gone, pulled up through
a funnel, little town in the sky.

MARTINA IN THE BADLANDS

Just the kind of place you can find a cold
hot dog and a flat soda.
A minute arrested me.

Across the large road American cars
swerved around jackrabbits. The sky blackened

near noon, hail big as hail.
We'll need a place to hide, she said.
I pulled out the Polaroid to shoot

a rainbow limping towards Miles City.
For her, I'm afraid

nothing else remained of the season.
I was either
Tim or Paul or Jim Holt.

How It Came to Be Connecticut

Local weather followed her everywhere.
Over a hill a dreamy white powder
encrusted the rim of a gypsum mine.
After four weeks in the northwest corner
it was a bad start. Clearings aren't what
they're cracked up to be: A vulture flew
concentric rings above our patch of dirt.
How it came to be Connecticut nobody knows.
All day we gathered brush, fallen limbs.
A goodly fire we made after dark, how it
carved mad shadows in her face. We'll
build, she said, pointing her fork at the night
beyond our camplight. Garage for the truck,
an attic for antlers. People come from all
over the world to the City, to begin again.
Then they come here looking for a little plot
in the wind, when they're done making a mess.
They'll never get this, she hissed, stabbing
her fork in the ground. It was about time
for me to head out. I have a cozy little crib
off the highway, and miles to go,
and sodium pentothal in case I dummy up.

A LOFT

A little blue space in the clouds
sails like a wink above
Mrs. Kane's laundry. It's gone.
A clash of ridges all week
rides the atmosphere. Let the rain
be your umbrella, teletype
relaying the infinite's inchings.

It's the Civil War all over.
Blame me. We made up presidents,
that's what front porches are for:
if the rocker is empty that must
mean that someone is off it.
Friday slouches on summer couches.
The hinges squeak like a cat.

In the room now a darker room
where scavengers have made fast,
bundled like raccoons on a job.
The news lines the shoes of Old Man
Steal Away, Mr. Pinch of Salt.
Those musty attic beams are soft,
Jackie Boy, rafters in a cloud.

PARADISE CITY

Tough to gauge which moves
quicker: clouds, or our blue planet
as it rounds on the next instant.
The velocity I experienced
seated on a park bench was
scarcely enough even to ruffle
my windbreaker. Drop-outs
were kicking hacky-sack in
front of General Pulaski's
plaque at lunchtime (though
'drop-out' might be dead
coinage), if they were really
drop-outs at all, and not just
idle rich kids who'd swapped
clothes in a Goodwill box. That
would be unacceptable. My
sandwich was gone. The faithful
poured out of the Church of Body
Modification as a good gust
from Canada unparted the minister's
hair. Something was hooked
in her eyebrow, something feathery,
suspicious, like a fishing lure.
I was alone and needed a plan.

DIORAMA

The biker at rest near the war memorial
calls me over: "I have this
little farm in my hands, see. Ma's
in the kitchen tinkering with a starter
she pulled off the John Deere.
There's one light on. Kerosene,
griddle cakes. She's craning her neck
over coils of copper wire like a jeweler,
grease thumbed under her eye."
I look in his hands because I have to
and there it all is, a weathervane
and a sundown sky, a wake of
chickens fluttering aside as the truck
pulls away trailing dust over the fields,
dust the boy calls smoke, the boy
with a nosebleed, his head tipped back.

BIG RECTANGULAR SMILE

In Brazil a bird will sit all day
on your shoulder. In Germany
this seldom happens. A hot-air
balloon luffs on convection currents
like a blowsy unmasted sail
though luff might not
mean what I mean. It could be
I'm going after bluff, if only
I could tell what the cards read.
On certain days everyone accuses me
of beastly things, creature
manipulated by subtle atmospheric
influences. A party-line chatters
wee helpless in the all hours.
Right now the bird is my stand-in.
He tells you where to put your clothes,
what homework to do. He kind of
speaks German, with a big rectangular
smile, as birds of Brazil often do.

44 IN A SCHOOL ZONE

So here on this rusty trestle
I started out. By then
the 2:15 was rolling down at last,
an honest-to-god steam engine
spitting venom. Or an image
of a locomotive lugging a spray of
soot behind it like a thought-
balloon. Far below the trestle
a summer day was in progress:
a reflection of kids splashing
in the water splashed apart
by kids splashing in the water.
Maybe they spotted me up there
clutching notes and hoped I'd do
anything, jump, break up a
perfectly eventless afternoon,
the kind that, in the temperate
zone, never ends, and make of it
a summer to remember,
but only in a general way.

THERE'S NO NOW

I'm trying to avoid
saying what I usually say
in these circumstances.
Are those real palm trees?
You're sitting on my hat.
Honestly, I've never been
lost—I always know
the correct turn eventually
will pop up. That's why
I'm here before you
and not where I should
be, which is a northern
climate, with only a few
war-era trees, some goats,
and a gramophone in good
working order. I get
funny at the mention of it.
Best just to keep driving,
looking for all the spots
where everyone else goes.
Remember steel piers?
How on Armistice Day
kids ran around grabbing
and stomping on everyone's

straw hats? That was before
my time, though my time
seems before my time. Except
when I double back, north
of Newark, to my hometown,
that's when I see my time's
long after my time, that we're
not likely to see my time
coming down the pike any time
soon, and if we did—
Yes, look, that *is* my hat.

ii.

[PLACE UNKNOWN]

It was a two-story duck on the side
of the highway. A greenglass insulator.
It was a derby under construction.
It was a zeppelin, old mother's shoe.
A giant had left his things behind.
The pavement made an enormous room.
Ancient Land of the Broken Nose.
It was a stucco accordion, a battleship
on dry land. It was a pop bottle
inside of which labored Mom & Pop.
It was an ark among the petunias,
with living babies, an iceberg in the desert.
The sky had dropped its huge sombrero.
It was a chili bowl flanked by a flight
of stairs. Tap dancers in the hoosegaw.
I Bring Good News, spake the handbill.

A PLAN OF HOW TO CATCH AMANDA

Then it dawned on me how easy it is
to lose one's way, to forget
the novelty of certain inventions, to cross
the beltway that cinches the district.
You might think what you see is a plan.
But count on this: people move away,
evidence disappears, memory fades.
If, leaving Scranton at dawn, I reach
Columbus by four and get out of my car
for a snack and a stroll in the neighborhoods,
if I fall into conversation with a retired
grocer sitting on a stoop, if he invites me
over to Mike's for a beer, if Mike's is run
by the grocer's high school chum who likes to
gamble and there's a horse race on TV
and a jar of pig feet at the other end and
a card game in the back that's almost
nine years old, if my reluctance to leave
before everyone else has left keeps me
until closing and I sleep an enchanted sleep
upon Mike's pool table, if it's already
tomorrow and my plans are receding
like a Greyhound into the vanishing point
of Interstate 70, if I walk the streets

of Columbus forever, doing tall headwork,
in search of my car, if the new plan
involves a rooming house and small change
sweeping up at the barber shop, if the tune
I punch into the juke box is the one
I used to listen to back east (even
when I don't remember this) so that what
I circle back to I don't recognize,
if after looking up from the classifieds
I ask a stranger directions and I am
distracted momentarily by a Goodyear
blimp floating pleasantly out to the stadium
and I turn back to the stranger, I'll put it
to him gently, asking him thus—

Also Known As

I was tall, moody, with a black handkerchief
draped across my face,

a salesman after dark.

I was optimistic, the guy in a pinch
who snips the right wire.

I saw hay bending under a western wind.
The land had been in the family for generations.

Then the family was in the land.

I remained optimistic. No one owned the mayor.
Optimism was a lonely office.

The previous mystic blew through here years back,
when our population was at its peak—

a courtly gentleman with jaundice.

I had shirts delivered to me from Corsica,
with buttons like little crossbows.

I was somewhat shorter than I appeared on the big screen,

at home in the great opera houses of the West.

Uncomfortable around flowers.

I disappeared for weeks at a time, riding fence,
a subway map in my vest pocket.

It isn't easy being short.
I think a lot of people overlook that.

We passed the vanishing point some time ago.

WIND SHEAR

Fill me in: Our estimated
time of arrival, was it taken
off the big board? This may
not matter if where we're
headed for isn't there when we
get there. Some rocky air
could ditch all my plans,
I'll tell ya. Microbursts are
violent downdrafts and hard
to detect. I landed once
in the most radiant city
and slept a week, while my
career spun out of control
and took my love-life
with it. I remember a comedy
club, a suspicion I'd had
that someone put something
in my drink. The patrons
seemed a little too friendly.
The walls I bumped into
sounded hollow, like a movie-
set. Everything needed ad-
justing: the woman's lipstick
smeared to not look like

a calculation, a scripted
randomness; the half-drunk-
from cocktail glasses fogged
with fingerprints in order
to refract the neon glare.
I wasn't there, I argued with
no one. Even the panhandlers
were in town only for a spare
convention. On a dare, I scaled
one of the non-indigenous trees.
When I let go, as proof,
it was a kind of flying.

MUCH LATER

And I went along, living on
crackers and pop, up and
down God's burnt-out road.
The jokes we told kept
getting lost in the wind.
In the distance I spied
a farmer's wife chasing white
bed sheets in a hayfield.
I was a hat she'd never
catch. Clouds like aprons
full of rock salt visited us.
A rusted Cat's Paw sign
hinged on groaning iron.
Hector was trying to tell me
something, something urgent
in the way he aimed his chin.
I couldn't get it. He was lost
like a radio wave. Smiley
nodded tragically toward
where the wind was going,
taking everything with it,
a pre-worn shirt snapping
around his scarecrow shoulders.

It's a Long Story so Let's Not Tell It

There was a two-way mirror
everyone stood on one side of.
A hotel with no doorknobs.

Behind bulletproof glass a clerk
counted ones,
though you wanted to say twenties.

A skinny girl cartwheeled across the grass at dusk.

Her daddy was a closetful of coats
with shoes underneath.

A remarkable sequence of events
was unlikely to occur or we were in one
without knowing it.

We were walking through a ghost town.
All the people were there too.

They had ghosts. They had rakes
and lime. Currency
passed between the living and the not-

so-living and the line
separating them was floating
and hard to pin down.

My Kind Is Unconnected

No evidence of foul play: all the guns
had been locked away. A coffee cup sat
in a chipped saucer next to the sink,
a crescent moon kissed on the rim.
I made a note. The guy didn't know
what hit him. Neither did we.
We didn't know what hit us either.
It's the 'fog of reality,' I guess,
that makes apprehending difficult,
how composites never equal the real
thing. Only at the retirement party
years later, did the captain admit
he was "stumped," and it was too bad,
wasn't it, we fingered the guy in 3C.
Everything fell into the wrong hands:
the water rights, the race-track
winnings, the blonde (who, I reminded
the captain, had been my wife).
Sure the track star had big feet,
that didn't mean he was going anywhere.
And if the wig had been admitted
during trial, we'd be singing a different
tune now, not the one on everyone's lips
nobody knows the words to,

the one I was humming last night
as I pressed the slacks of my only
good suit, the one I heard
my neighbor whistling at the boarding
house as he was loading his revolver—
Wait a minute, Captain.
I think it's coming back to me.

IDIOT MEANS GOOD LUCK

Too bad the storm cellar could fit all of us
but one. A little boy cried, Everybody! Maybe
it was possible. Pretty Polly had disappeared
through a fence hole with the propane man.
A sandwich wrapper blew across the tracks.
The purple structure looking like a whorehouse
at the end of Old Main had no cellar at all,
just sat there on the ground like a fallen woman.
Stand barefoot in the middle of the living room
and you'd feel the grave cold of the earth
rise through your soles, March wind balled under
the joists, the ground frozen well into spring.
Tornadoes were rare in that neck of the woods.
Still, storm cellars were considered good insurance.
But the sky was tricky, like being in Albany
on April Fool's Day, brightening out of nowhere,
all that modern concrete leaning against nothing,
politicians waiting for the light to change, the striped
crosswalks, zones of immunity, suggestions really,
and a stiff wind that comes from all across New
York State to rough up a hot dog vendor. The pols
at lunch tool plans for the river, denying everything
they said yesterday. A cast iron bridge spans
the river south of the city, changing color as daylight

shifts, and I dream of crossing it; by nightfall
it's glowing, reefers barreling westward.
What river is that, I said, pointing, and the boy,
the same boy, answered wistfully, The Ganges. A very
good answer, I told him, but wrong. I remember
Thanksgiving dinner at the whorehouse, interrupting
the Madame's toast, I couldn't stop talking, it was
strange, I accepted that; I seemed to be on the verge
of explaining something, but I lost what came next.
A consensus had emerged, well nearly a consensus,
as the twister loomed over the Howard's dairy farm,
about who would be left outside. It was a problem,
I tried to convince them as I pounded on the bulkhead,
for which there could never be an ideal solution.

CINCO DE MAYO, VIRGINIA

The late bus pulled in late. Honest.
An auspicious start for some rummy.
He listened and sipped a warm beer.
He looked like where secrets are saved.
A pool of darkness was spreading out
down in the hollow. Here's a tip:
End-of-the-Line in the eighth.
Do you long for furlong? The question
kept him moving from town to town—
an unspoken demand of the genre.
A farmer was the only one on hand.
The smooth wreck of midnight was
coming in for a landing, a terrestrial
event involving hayfields and stuck
landing gear. Light fell from clouds.
She was five feet four inches
of smoke and mirrors, part time
lapidary, spur track on the long run.
We're an optimistic people, she said,
despite the evidence. We're always there
to lend a hand or look the other way.
We're always there, after the bus leaves,
and the stores close, and the judge
climbs the stairs with his cat. To us

it matters what the mailman thinks.
We're not strangers, she said strangely.
You're safe, I'll never see you again.
Let me tell you a secret, said she—

EEYORE'S INSOMNIA ROTISSERIE

We came up just a bit short. No
one thought we'd come up at all.
A boyhood hero towered above us,
biting a corn dog. To me he was
the hungriest member of the tribe.
Hooligans spread a picnic blanket
in his shade, crushing Dr. Peppers.
Summer days were endless, even after
I went home; likely endless
summer days for those who remained,
to revel in them and drag them out.
Glee can only be stretched so far until
it becomes something else, a drum-
tight alibi, a weird prophylactic.
Of cannibals crossing the desert—
all but one or two will survive.
In the shade of our boyhood hero
the days were always short. The sun
hid behind his hat, faking twilight.
Birds stopped singing in the middle
of the day, flowers closed up shop.
Summer moved on to some misty
real estate beyond, isle of lost toys,
off-season amusement park
where a ride paused to lift us up.

Due West

It's not like it was
all bad the place
she lived. Still
if she could endure

she thought the knotted
road thousands rode
everyday she might wind-up
somewhere else.

Halfway there stands
an American
elm on the plain
cooling fevered

travelers who'd not lost
their way since all they
knew was direction.
The landscape inscribed

distance in their looks.
Because there was a here
and a here after that
she was willing to range.

Slept Here. Moved On.

Washington slept one night in this little museum.
What a strange man he must've been.
In those days there was so much less
that was old and could be saved.

The candle-flame sputtered in its dish.
He bid goodnight to the nice lady.
Each night new rafters, new bible on the pillow.
Such dark country to be traveling alone.

Wherever he went became a monument.
Washington, who kindly lay in any bed
offered him, with that famous
wooden jaw-line, reclining, thank you ma'am,

stiffly upon his back, eyelids
clattering shut. Even his horse, stoic,
propped up in a stable, enduring flies.
Brave horse minted on the back of a coin.

GHOST 66

A mare's tail brushes over Indiana.
Go-karts on Sunday fly around
the figure-eight. Plywood Arc de Triomphe
and a cyclone fence. Powerlines make
a margin at the bottom of the sky—a staff,
Little Birds, and you are the notes
when the wind comes, and it does.
If we could only harness such power,
dreams the cook at Steak 'n' Shake.
It could happen. He saw tray girls,
and there were tray girls, roller skates
on the lone prairie, and lunch came sailing
over fresh macadam with a smile.
It's no mirage, stranger, this dirt is
a town. Gaze out the picture window,
picture where you're headed: the horizon,
then more horizon, swallowed by dusk.
Then more horizon, and a wallet.

iii.

ACCUMULATION

A speck of dust is the seed of a snowflake.
So it was that dust built a blizzard.
While you were out the blizzard posted signs,

lost dog hounding your footsteps.
Something in the newspaper about it.

Let the houses be known for the people who left them.

Snow settled upon a hat, making a fort.
Snow traveled all this way
to make itself something to keep itself in.

Bowl of blue shade.

The dog thought he could, by circling,
conjure a yard and put his people in it.
The way a speck of dust conjures a dog.

Here comes the moment he's been waiting for.
Here comes the one after that.

EVERYTHING'S JAKE

You never know. And even if you do,
you don't know. A young man
in summer steals a pick-up and gets
a blow-out doing fifty on a dirt road
beside infinite cornfields. Hot
blue sky yawning above the country-
side, fractional day-moon inching
along like a turtle on a sheet of glass.
You never know. Gee, he thinks, wish
I had a girlfriend. I wish I was
driving with her in an Oldsmobile,
summer evening, windows down,
radio loud. But even in dreams
something goes wrong. A gust of wind
blasts through the car, snatching
the money folded in his shirt pocket,
scattering it over Monroe County.
And he's stuck combing the roadside
up to his knees in mystery
grass, and night's fallen hard,
and in the time it takes to fix a flat
his girl hitches back to Livonia.

Livingston County

August, a night of freak cold. Rosemary takes notes. The top leaves of her rock maple have turned fire orange, a flag...*Some western rust*, she writes. *I see a storm on the way, far off, the size of a man*...He hops off a flatbed truck and flips an apple core over an electric fence. He doesn't seem to know what to do with himself. *Blackbirds light on a high tension line*, she writes, *wind jangled wire*. Rosemary is the prettiest woman in town. She can say anything she wants. One day at the post office, she looked up from the zip code directory and smiled at me. The next evening I came close to knocking on her door but then I heard her cough inside. *There's a break in the clouds at sunset*, she writes. *A red window*....

EVE WITH THE LID ON

We can cheap it back that far.
By now the coast is clear.
With a bad night's sleep behind us
the rest stop fades away.
Still things happen all the time:
vapor trails in tatters,
plastic rain forest creatures
rallying on the dashboard.
A shoebox decimated by winter reposes
in an open field:
inside: a mitten, a broken tooth
worth an almost extinct
two-dollar bill:
an expedition to the interior
of the interior. The shadow range
claimed another party.
A secret agent in short pants
rattled ice; the pets had
a little caged-in area where
they could get acquainted.
Mr. Goat, with flat goat looks,
a jaunty underbite,
I make of this cap a gift.
I make of this map a legend:

no one will know you, spy lad,
that's the way to travel.

Spark Gap

Helicopter circling over town—
someone's missing. We're in unfamiliar
territory. One night
a lady jumped up out of my backyard
fixing her skirt, explaining
there was absolutely nothing
I could do. Sooner or later
I'd be called upon to make a leap.
There was an unlit path for me
to cover, a clearing
where plays were staged.
I sat one season in close
company for the third act.
By then it was summer.
We were lit. A guard
making rounds at the asylum
whistled across the river. Years
later, patients loafing down-
town near the bus stop,
I heard that tune again.
This is how a tree girdles,
I tell my boys, one root squeezes off
the other roots. This is where
that lady jumped out, I say,
picking up my shovel.

A Day Unlike Any Other

When Rutherford B. Hayes comes to town,
squirrels are charmed out of the eaves.
The editor breaks down and sobs.
It's a rare day. So rare we almost want it back.
But we give it to Mr. Hayes, the man
elected by the skin of his teeth.
We honor his teeth. We wish he were king.
We live in a different world, the right world,
the world of mules and Rutherford B. Hayes.
Our inventory of beards has been replenished.
His unrecorded remarks fill the air.
It's impossible to breathe, without breathing
the ether around him. He's the world's
slowest speaker. He addressed us yesterday,
and look here, he addresses us today.
Our township rises on his tide.
The police sleep the sleep of the innocent;
the river is sweet, the catfish mighty.

HARD TIMES

Every day he watched his feet when he walked and every day they seemed a little more distant. One day entering an ice cream shop he looked down and sure enough it was like his feet, shod in penny-loafers, were telescoping away from him. The sky too had been changing lately, and not for the better, getting slightly closer, and on those days of high pressure, the blue sky seemed a little less blue. And the trees, weren't they taller once? When did they start looking stunted, like charcoal sketches drawn by a disturbed child? And the shade was cooler in 1952, and what about in the 1800s, when we knew how to live? That was when a boy and his horse could really be shod. He remembered the heaviness of brogans, loafing along a mountain road in high summer, and locusts humming in the giant trees, and in one hand he was clutching a bouquet of wildflowers for someone, and in the other, a stick of dynamite.

Reconstruction

Through some unfinished framework
more framework is visible.
A fox minces across fluke snow.
New detours baffle the locals.
It started with a plant in a window,
a decal of sunshine. What they
made up was what they were made
of. It's a little world, after all,
with lots of big worlds in it.
The disappearance of an indigenous
songbird worries merchants,
though its song turns up somewhat
later with fifth graders
clustered below a brimming levee.
An armadillo from out of time
nestles like a tintype among
useful things. How well he misses
what he knew of Sweetwater,
a crossroad he counts on crossing.

LEADS

That Rodney kited checks and bought an Indian
motorcycle and rode it west. That he lived upstairs
practicing his penmanship in a one-window room.
That the pewter candy dish on the mantle
was a wedding present for someone else. That
drought would take its toll on the spring peepers.
That in the mill section of town a fire was
doused; that it reappeared outside the druggist's,
who refused to unlock his doors. That the fire-
house itself was the scene of some unnerving
shadows. That a man on a bet leapfrogged
every parking meter between Gothic and Crafts.
That in a window of the judge's house a girl
nightly fixed her hair. That from the street
it was impossible to tell if she was singing or
chewing gum. That burning iron illuminated the sky
over six states. That every spring turned up ghosts
in the garden: doll heads, broken dinner plates.
That in a nearby hollow hoboes cooked mulligan,
and the cuckoo warbled on Independence Day.
That the earth casts a red shadow. That folks pass
through here to a bigger place. That a rumor
circulated of a map stashed in the foundation,
a map of secret routes to the heartland, which was

suspect, but by then the rumor had taken hold.
That white shirts on hangers would appear
among the dogwoods. That a trail of candy wrappers
could lead nowhere in particular. That the swift
harbored a secret that would have to remain
a secret. That in a distant county fans followed
baseball by Morse code. That when a child
tosses crumbs into the sky, the stars throw them back
down. That upon entering the house Jack would say
the closer I get, the farther I can see.

THERE

How good it is to be there, or anywhere.
When I was there yesterday, I was really
there, all there, limbs, credit cards.
I was there last week but I didn't have
all my things. My glasses were off and so
was my timing. What I meant to bring there
I'd left somewhere else, which is where I think of
when I think of what it's like to be all there.
I never wake in my right mind,
not all of it. Some part is right, I'll concede,
the part that makes concessions;
the rest is there, where I left it, wrong.
Margaret brings tea and says I don't seem
all there. I say that's because I was
all there yesterday and some parts didn't make it
back for today. If I return there for
the parts I left there I may find I'm again
all there, as far as an inventory goes, the parts
laid out on an oilcloth and accounted for,
all there, but not in the form I'm accustomed to.

Bird Throat, Calabash, Glove Oil

We had a little catch in the morning.
A knot of traffic was tied
two blocks away. Aweigh, too,
as in, raise the anchor.
Away we go. We had a little more
catch, and the pitches went wild.
Bells were ringing on mountain day.
Venus in the waking world
in high tops. An anchorite
passed, bearing bread. We heard
chains catching as another launch
gave the heave-ho. Remarkable too
in the old world of today, I thought,
were the candy-stripers engaged
in starched devotionals,
hand-holding at the crosswalk.
The book was opened, and somebody
was reading it, but to whom?

KIND OF A STRANGE FEW MINUTES

All afternoon it felt like
someone was coming from miles off

down Mill River. I'd built
a serviceable lookout

of toothpicks with a secret
door in the back through which

some miniature soldiers
could escape. It was bound

to be slow-going for them,
what with a landscape of rubber

centipedes, spoon-dug fossil
sites, and our neighbor

the mole uneasy
among dandelions and crabgrass,

blinking back daylight.
A message had to get through.

The soldiers, led by the vigilant

Captain General, crouching, single-

minded, taking aim,
will find a way out: a storm-

drain, a culvert,
a riverbank, a rowboat

to sail off in—
clouds like smeared pencilings,

a mysterious erasure
taking place over their heads.

LANE OF BLUE MIST

I ventured over to the exit ramp
and pitched rocks into a drainage ditch,
tired of looking safe for a ride.
A red wing unfolded on the pavement.
Oxbow, sluicegate. Farmhands
took me in, fed me. On the plate was
drawn a peasant woman pushing a cart
loaded with corn. A little dog yapped
between her steps. Red August dust.
A pack of ravens dallied in the hemlocks.
Rake clatter, wind grip, rail path, trestle.
I miss the comet tailing above
the Industrial Park. Lights that fell
over the graveyard were never explained,
thank goodness. A packet's unmoored
though no current carries it off.

ALBERTA CLIPPER

Washboard shadow, the clapboard at 5 PM. Later, the man who haunts the Coolidge house dials the sheriff. A cigarette ember in the window glowers like a pilot light. Among night-trees sniffs a no-good dog. Crescent moon so crisp we see the outline of what's unseen. The usual skull-thought follows. How light, a newborn's head weighted on the palm, its first bath, a winter night, snow that goes on for miles... When exiting a room it's best to let the music play itself out. Django in the woods of Europe between the wars. Django with a fish.

I'VE GOT PEOPLE IN TOWN

When I woke up it was years later.
My cigar had gone out.
A wing chair stood in a corner of a trailer
in lower Florida, from which I arose,
my tweed suit unsuitable for July.
I stepped outside onto a milk crate.
My neighbor adored me. It was the Fourth,
and she went on washing dishes,
winking over a flowerbox of plastic gladiolus.
I was hoping for a long afternoon.
The sea-green petals of her housedress trembled
like postage stamps from a small country.
Blue mussel shells smoldered in the driveway,
heat shimmying off the guardrail.
My shadow snuck back under my shoes.
A Volkswagen sat at the curb,
the People's Car. And at the wheel
my trusted guide, Wendell, to whom
I also dictate. Dear Floridians, I began,
I will need more money, and my dog.

ACKNOWLEDGMENTS

American Letters & Commentary, Barrow Street, Black Warrior Review, Conduit, Crazyhorse, Crying Sky, FIELD, 5AM, Gettysburg Review, Green Mountains Review, LIT, Margie, Open City, Poetry Daily, Pool, Quarterly West, Slope, Verse Daily, Washington Square.

Some of these poems also appeared in the chapbook, A Plan of How to Catch Amanda, published by Factory Hollow Press, 2007.

Other Titles
from The National Poetry Review Press

Lucktown by Bryan Penberthy

Bill's Formal Complaint by Dan Kaplan

Gilgamesh at the Bellagio by Karl Elder

Grace by Degrees by Dorine Jennette

The Kissing Party by Sarah E. Barber

Please visit our website for more information:

www.nationalpoetryreview.com

www.ingramcontent.com/pod-product-compliance
Lightning Source LLC
Chambersburg PA
CBHW022031090426